S0-BFC-118

CRICKET

Garden Minibeasts UP CLOSE

John Woodward

CHELSEA CLUBHOUSE
An Imprint of Chelsea House Publishers

Cricket

Chelsea Clubhouse
An imprint of Chelsea House
132 West 31st Street
New York, NY 10001

Library of Congress Cataloging-in-Publication Data
Woodward, John, 1954-
  Cricket : garden minibeasts up close / John Woodward.
      p. cm. -- (Garden minibeasts up close)
  Includes bibliographical references and index.
  ISBN 978-1-60413-902-0
  1. Crickets--Juvenile literature. I. Title. II. Series: Woodward, John, 1954- Garden minibeasts up close.
  QL508.G8W66 2010
  595.7'26--dc22

                           2010007237

Chelsea Clubhouse books are available at special discounts when purchased in bulk quantities for businesses, associations, institutions, or sales promotions. Please call our Special Sales Department in New York at (212) 967-8800 or (800) 322-8755.

You can find Chelsea Clubhouse on the World Wide Web at http://www.chelseahouse.com

Produced for Chelsea House by Discovery Books
Managing Editor: Laura Durman
Project Editor: Clare Collinson
Designer: Blink Media
Illustrator: Bernard Thornton/John Francis

Photo acknowledgments: FLPA: pp 10 (Panda Photo), 16 (Michael Durham/Minden Pictures), 19 (L. Lee Rue), 22 (Panda Photo), 27 (Piotr Naskrecki/Minden Pictures); Getty Images: p 18 (Jeff Foott); iStockphoto.com: title page (craftvision), pp 4 (Steve Geer), 7 (Samuli Siltanen), 8 (Tom Hahn), 9 (constantgardener), 15 top (Jennifer Foeller), 17 (Jacob Hamblin), 25 (Cathy Keifer), 26 (Craig Cozart), 29 (kostas koutsoukos); Photoshot: pp 20 (Bruce Coleman), 21 (Maik Dobiey), 23 (Woodfall Wild Images), 28 (Edward L. Snow); Shutterstock Images: pp 5 (ahnhuynh), 11 (Bruce MacQueen), 12 and 13 (Liew Weng Keong), 14 (Cathy Keifer), 15 bottom (SVT Photography), 24 (orionmystery@flickr).

Cover printed by Bang Printing, Brainerd, MN
Book printed and bound by Bang Printing, Brainerd, MN
Date printed May 2010
Printed in the United States of America

10 9 8 7 6 5 4 3 2 1

This book is printed on acid-free paper.

Contents

Finding crickets

The best way to find crickets is to listen for them! You can often hear their musical chirping calls on warm evenings in late spring and summer.

Most crickets spend the day hiding in burrows or under stones, logs, or leaves. They come out at night to feed.

Crickets are insects that you will sometimes see feeding on flowers and other plants in backyards.

4

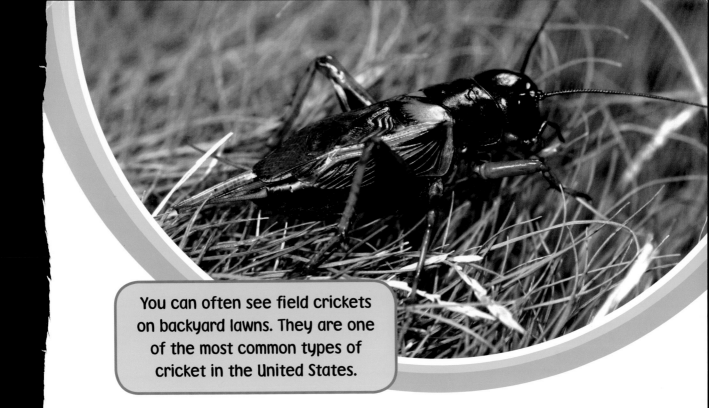

You can often see field crickets on backyard lawns. They are one of the most common types of cricket in the United States.

Did You Know?

You may have crickets living in your home! House crickets prefer to live indoors. Some field crickets sneak into houses in cold weather, too. The best time to look for them is at night when they come out to feed. They gobble up any crumbs and scraps they can find.

If you hear a cricket chirping, see if you can find it. Walk slowly or it will leap away! If it's singing in the grass, it's likely to be a field cricket or a ground cricket. If it's in a tree, it's a tree cricket. And if it's in a bush, then it's probably a bush cricket!

A cricket's body

Would you know a cricket if you saw one? Most adult crickets have brown, black, or green bodies that are about an inch long. Like all insects, they have six legs. Their two back legs are usually much longer than the other four.

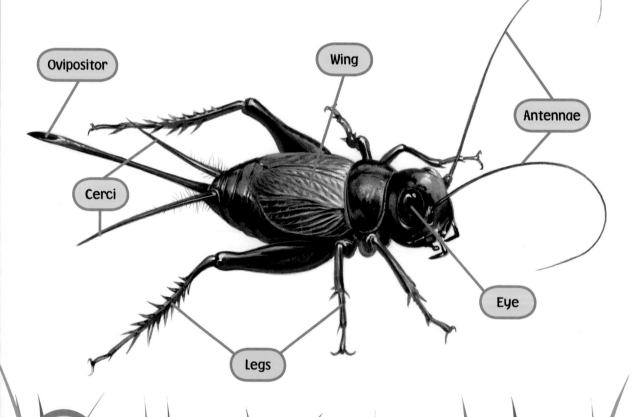

Ovipositor

Wing

Antennae

Cerci

Legs

Eye

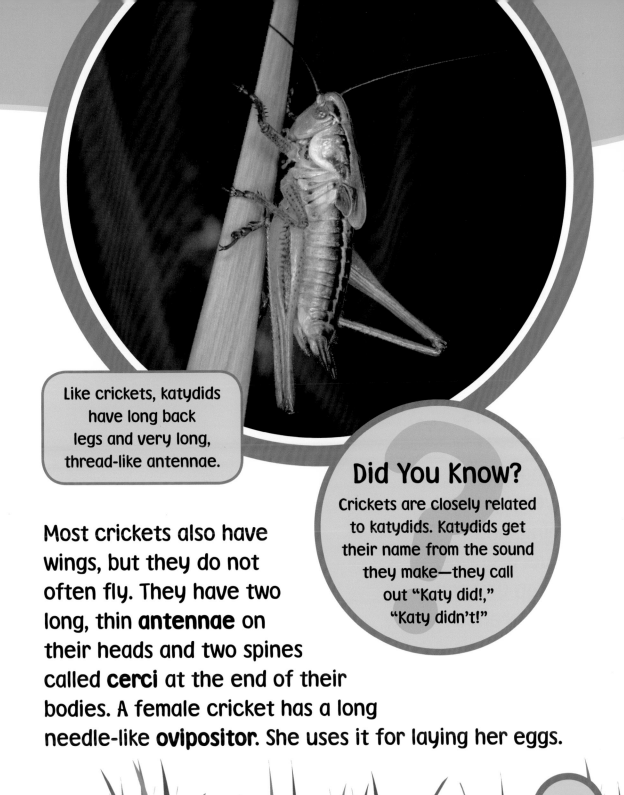

Like crickets, katydids have long back legs and very long, thread-like antennae.

Did You Know?
Crickets are closely related to katydids. Katydids get their name from the sound they make—they call out "Katy did!," "Katy didn't!"

Most crickets also have wings, but they do not often fly. They have two long, thin **antennae** on their heads and two spines called **cerci** at the end of their bodies. A female cricket has a long needle-like **ovipositor.** She uses it for laying her eggs.

The cricket family

Crickets and katydids belong to a large group of insects that also includes **grasshoppers**. Like crickets, grasshoppers are very good at jumping, and they look very similar. How can you tell the difference?

Like crickets, grasshoppers have long back legs. But look at this grasshopper's antennae. They are much shorter than a cricket's antennae.

The best way to tell them apart is to look at their antennae. Crickets have long antennae that look like cotton threads. Grasshoppers have short, stiff antennae.

Did You Know?

There are at least 22,000 different types of crickets, katydids, and grasshoppers in the world. Of these, about 1,000 kinds live in North America.

Female grasshoppers also have much shorter ovipositors than female crickets.

Grasshoppers usually sing during the day rather than in the evening. They make buzzing calls that sound less musical than the chirping songs of crickets.

You can often see grasshoppers feeding on plants in backyards.

9

Chirping calls

Have you ever watched a cricket singing? How does it make its chirping call? Crickets sing by rubbing their front wings against each other. Each kind of cricket makes a different pattern of chirps.

Did You Know?

Like crickets, katydids make their calls by rubbing their front wings together. Grasshoppers make their buzzing sounds by scraping their legs against their wings.

To make its musical chirps, a cricket holds its wings open and rubs one of its front wings against the bumpy edge of the other wing.

10

Usually it is only male crickets that sing. They make loud calls to attract females and warn off other males. They sing very quietly during **courtship**, when a female is near.

Did You Know?

If you listen to a snowy tree cricket chirping, you will be able to tell the temperature! Snowy tree crickets chirp more quickly when they are warmer. Count the number of chirps the cricket makes in 13 seconds and add 40. This will give you the temperature in degrees Fahrenheit.

Cricket senses

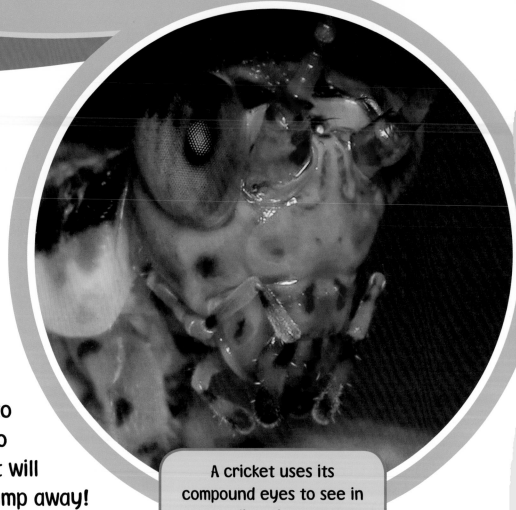

A cricket uses its compound eyes to see in many directions at the same time.

If you try to get close to a cricket, it will probably jump away! How does it know you are there? Crickets have very good vision. They have **compound eyes**, made up of lots of tiny **lenses**.

Crickets use their long antennae to detect smells and to feel their way around in the dark. A cricket also has special hairs on the cerci at the end of its body. These help the cricket feel air movements that might mean an enemy is nearby.

Did You Know?

Crickets and katydids have good hearing, but if you look at their heads you will not see any ears. Their ears are just below the knees on their front legs!

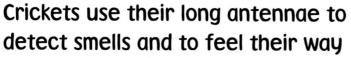

Ears

13

Enemies and defenses

Crickets are a favorite food of many different animals, such as spiders, bats, beetles, and birds. So how do crickets protect themselves from **predators**?

Crickets, grasshoppers, and katydids have lots of enemies, including spiders.

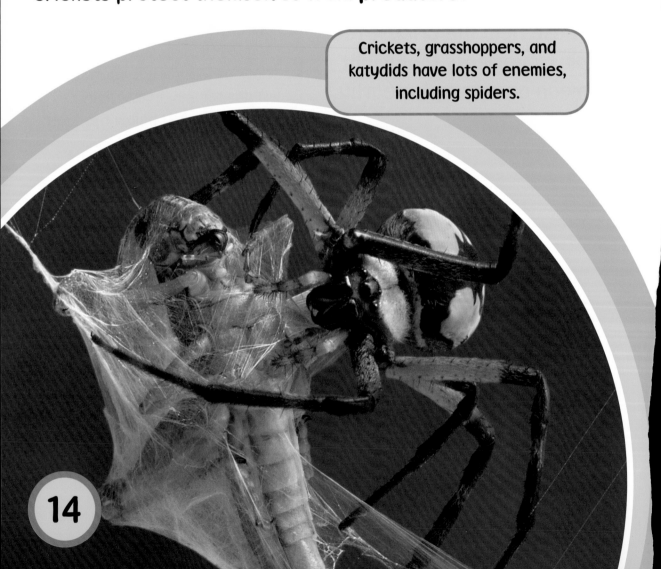

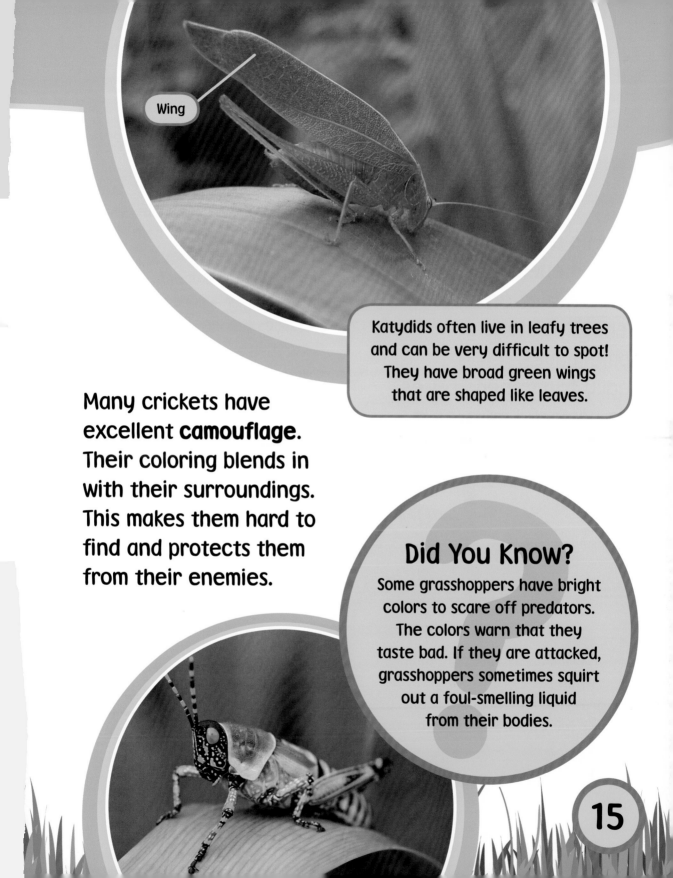

Wing

Katydids often live in leafy trees and can be very difficult to spot! They have broad green wings that are shaped like leaves.

Many crickets have excellent **camouflage**. Their coloring blends in with their surroundings. This makes them hard to find and protects them from their enemies.

Did You Know?

Some grasshoppers have bright colors to scare off predators. The colors warn that they taste bad. If they are attacked, grasshoppers sometimes squirt out a foul-smelling liquid from their bodies.

Jumping and flying

When a cricket senses that an enemy is nearby, it often hides beneath a stone or some leaves. If it is really frightened, it uses the powerful muscles in its back legs to quickly jump away.

Crickets usually only jump when they are in danger. For grasshoppers, hopping is one of their favorite ways to get around!

Mormon crickets have small wings, but they cannot fly. Instead, they just crawl and hop.

Many kinds of crickets can fly, but not very well! Some field crickets have small wings, and they cannot fly at all.

Grasshoppers are often much better at flying than crickets. Some can fly so well that they are known as "bird grasshoppers."

Mole and cave crickets

There are some kinds of cricket that you will hardly ever see. Mole crickets spend most of their lives in burrows underground. They feed on the roots of grasses and other plants.

Mole crickets use their large, claw-like front legs to dig burrows in lawns and fields.

18

Some crickets are known as "cave crickets" because they spend their lives in dark, damp places such as caves. They can sometimes be found hiding in basements, or under rocks or leaves.

Cave crickets have no ears and no wings, so they cannot hear or make chirping sounds. They use their long antennae to feel their way around and find food.

Food and feeding

Crickets eat almost any kind of plants they can find, and they don't just eat the leaves! They like to feed on seeds, fruits, flowers, and roots.

Like crickets, katydids have strong biting jaws, which they use to chew through their food.

This cricket has found a tasty tomato that has fallen to the ground.

Some crickets eat **fungi** and rotting plant material. House crickets feed mainly on crumbs and kitchen scraps. Other crickets, including tree crickets, are active hunters. They catch and eat other insects such as caterpillars.

Did You Know?

Crickets are sometimes **cannibals**. They eat dead crickets when there is no other food available. Sometimes they will even attack live ones!

21

Males and females

If you see a cricket, how can you tell if it is a male or a female? If you can hear it singing, it is probably a male. Female crickets are usually silent.

Did You Know?

Although most of the loud chirps and buzzes that you hear are produced by males, some female katydids and grasshoppers can sing, too. A male and female may even sing a **duet**!

A female cricket has heard the mating call of a male. The female is on the left. The male cricket is at the entrance to his burrow.

Like crickets, female katydids use their long ovipositors to lay eggs. This katydid is laying her eggs in the soil.

Male and female crickets usually **mate** in late summer. The females then look for a place to lay their eggs. They use their ovipositors to push the eggs into soil, plant stems, or tree bark. A female cricket lays up to 2,000 eggs during her life.

Did You Know?

Mating can be deadly for male Jerusalem crickets. After mating, female Jerusalem crickets often eat the males!

23

Growing up

Crickets usually hatch from their eggs in spring. Young crickets are called **nymphs**. A cricket nymph looks like a tiny version of its parents, but at first it has no wings. Female cricket nymphs do not have long ovipositors.

In springtime, you may be able to find some cricket nymphs in your backyard.

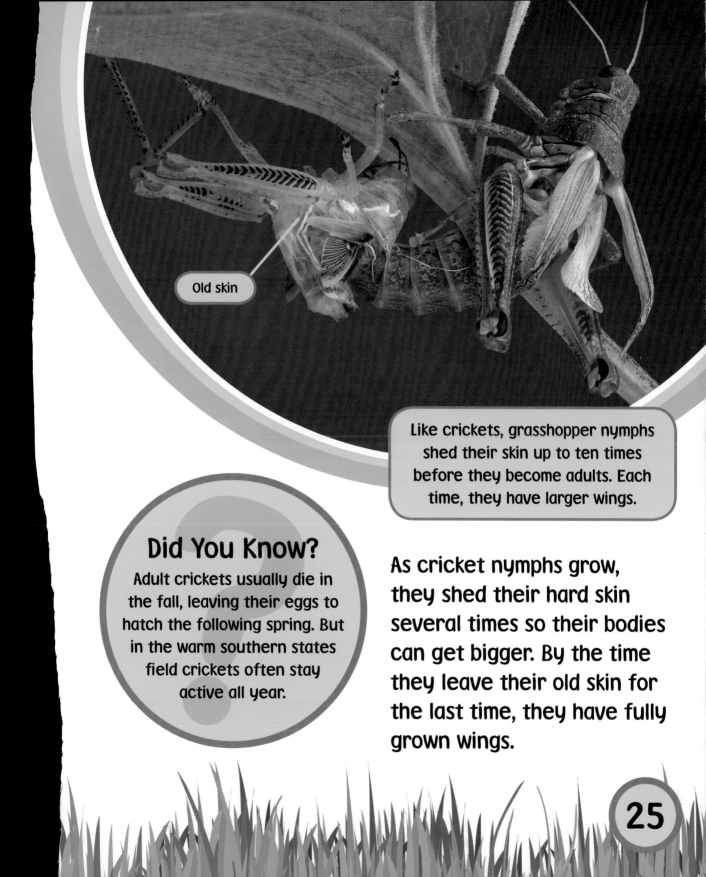

Old skin

Like crickets, grasshopper nymphs shed their skin up to ten times before they become adults. Each time, they have larger wings.

Did You Know?

Adult crickets usually die in the fall, leaving their eggs to hatch the following spring. But in the warm southern states field crickets often stay active all year.

As cricket nymphs grow, they shed their hard skin several times so their bodies can get bigger. By the time they leave their old skin for the last time, they have fully grown wings.

Swarms

Mormon crickets cannot fly, but they can crawl and hop long distances! Sometimes they form large groups called **swarms**, which may include millions of crickets.

The Mormon crickets in this swarm risk their lives crossing a road in Oregon. They can travel up to a mile a day.

Did You Know?

Mormon crickets are named after the Mormons, a religious group that settled in Utah. The Mormons' first crops were attacked by thousands of crickets. But the crops were saved when gulls moved in to the area and feasted on the crickets!

The swarms travel from one area to another looking for food. They often cause great damage to **crops** and other plants on their way.

Did You Know?

In Africa and the Middle East, desert locusts can form swarms of up to 50 billion insects, covering 400 square miles!

You may have heard the expression "a **plague** of locusts." Locusts are grasshoppers that **migrate** in big swarms. They can fly long distances in search of a good place to feed.

Swarming locusts may travel for several days before settling in a farmer's field. Once they have landed, they often eat the entire crop!

27

Crickets and people

Most people like to hear the chirping calls of crickets, but they also think that crickets can be pests. This is because crickets cause great damage to crops and other plants.

Crickets may damage plants in backyards, but they do an important job, too. The waste they produce helps to keep the soil healthy, so new plants can grow.

When you are near a cricket, hold your hand still. If you are lucky, it might jump onto your hand. Never pick a cricket up with your fingers. You might frighten it or damage it.

In some parts of the world, people have been keeping crickets as pets for hundreds of years. In Asia, people keep them in cages so they can listen to their musical songs. They are also thought to bring good luck to the home.

Did You Know?

Crickets have even featured as Walt Disney cartoon characters! Jiminy Cricket appeared in Disney's 1940 version of *Pinocchio* and Cri-Kee was a character in the 1998 Disney film *Mulan*.

Glossary

antennae: The "feelers" on the head of an insect, which it uses to feel its way around and to detect smells.

camouflage: A type of coloring or shape that makes something hard to see against its background.

cannibal: An animal that eats other animals of the same species.

cerci: The two hair-like, spiny structures at the end of a cricket's body.

compound eye: A bundle of many very simple eyes that act together to form a picture. All adult insects have this type of eye.

courtship: Behavior used by a male or female to attract a mate.

crop: On a farm, a plant that is grown in a field so it can be harvested.

duet: Two animals or people singing together.

fungi: Living things that look a little like plants but feed on the remains of other living things. Mushrooms and toadstools are fungi.

grasshopper: An insect related to a cricket, with the same jumping legs but much shorter antennae.

lenses: See-through structures in the eye that focus light to form pictures in the brain.

mate: When males and females come together to produce young.

migrate: In animals, to make a journey from one place to another, often to find food.

nymph: A young insect, after it has hatched from an egg and before it becomes an adult.

ovipositor: The sharp egg-laying tube at the end of the body of a female cricket, or other insect.

plague: In connection with insects, a vast number that gather together and often cause serious destruction.

predator: An animal that attacks and eats other live animals.

swarm: A group of many hundreds, thousands, or even millions of insects.

Further resources

Books

Elliott, Lang, and Wil Hershberger. *The Songs of Insects*. Boston: Houghton-Mifflin, 2007.
A book about the various types of crickets, with detailed photographs and a CD of their calls.

Gonzales, Doreen. *Crickets in the Dark*. New York: Rosen Publishing, 2010.
This book is full of information about these insects.

Hall, Margaret. *Crickets*. Mankato: Capstone Press, 2005.
An introduction to crickets, including their behavior and habits.

Hartley, Karen, Chris Macro, and Philip Taylor. *Grasshopper*. Chicago: Heinemann-Raintree, 2006.
An interesting introduction to grasshoppers.

Hibbert, Clare. *The Life of a Grasshopper*. Chicago: Heinemann-Raintree, 2004.
This book explains how a grasshopper develops from an egg into an adult insect. You can also find out where grasshoppers live and the animals that threaten them throughout their lives.

Slade, Suzanne. *Grasshoppers*. New York: Rosen Publishing, 2008.
An information-packed look at the grasshoppers that live in your backyard.

Web sites

Insecta-inspecta World, "Field Crickets", *http://www.insecta-inspecta.com/crickets/field/index.html*
A close look at one of the most common types of cricket, with a sound file and information about strange things such as cricket fighting!

The Singing Insects of North America, *http://entnemdept.ufl.edu/walker/buzz/index.htm*
An online identification guide to crickets. It includes both photographs and recordings of their chirping songs, so you can identify them by sight or sound.

The Songs of Insects, *http://www.musicofnature.com/songsofinsects/iframes/OLG_families.html*
An excellent online guide to insect songs, with photographs, sound recordings, and useful maps showing where the insects live.

Crickets, *http://www.biokids.umich.edu/critters/Gryllidae/*
This Web site gives interesting information and facts about crickets.

Cannibal Crickets, *http://www.sciencenewsforkids.org/articles/20060308/Note2.asp*
A Web page about Mormon crickets focusing on the fact that they like to eat each other.

Index